# FISHPONDS

1. The few shops on the left are the first travelling towards Fishponds, after Eastville Park. Watson Rust Newsagent, with next door a hairdresser, Fry's Chocolate and Lipton's Tea advertised.

2. The funeral of Rev. Melville Griffiths, moving down Fishponds Road, at the junction of Marlborough Road.

# FISHPONDS

3. Thingwall Park, a pleasant road between Huyton Road and Grove Road.

4. Parton and Co. Newsagent and Tobacconist on the corner of Grove Road and Fishponds Road. Card postally used January 1906.

# FISHPONDS

5. Regent Place on the corner of Fishponds Road and Alexandra Park. The Golden Lion public house first opened in 1866. The card posted in Fishponds in July 1906.

6. This view looking towards Eastville, the rank of shops on the corner of Brentry Road. Posted in May 1913 and published by Fred Viner of Weston-Super-Mare.

# FISHPONDS

7. A 1950's picture, Lodge Causeway, which connects from Thicket Avenue to Fishponds Road. Shops on the right include Cadle & Sons, and Bolloms Cleaners. Just in view on the right, the once familiar sight, a Brooke Bond tea van.

8. The Hillfields Park end of Lodge Causeway. The road in centre distance leading to Cossham Hospital, the junction on the right is Russell Road. Modern houses now replace many of the older houses. Card postally used 1904.

# FISHPONDS

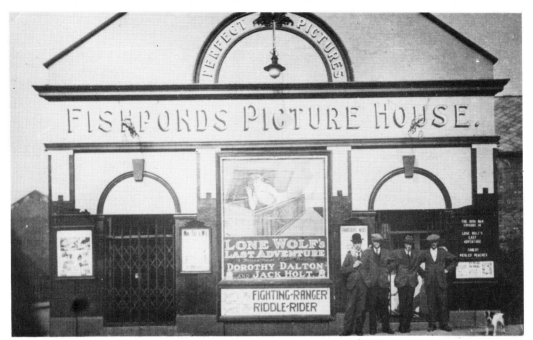

**9.** Fishponds Cinema. Built in 1911 on the corner of Station Avenue, one of the earliest silent cinema's, closed in the late 1920's, and is now Fishponds library.

**10.** Two trams near the junction with New Station Road, the Vandyke Cinema on the right which opened in 1929. Card published by the well known local shop Miltons.

# FISHPONDS

11. Lloyds Bank on the corner of Elmdale Gardens. Picture about 1908.

12. Fishponds Road. The rank of shops facing Lodge Causeway, with Elmgrove Post Office, with C. Stokes Chemist next door, who had branches in Fishponds and Stapleton Road. Tram no. 140 destination Fishponds from Tramway Centre.

# FISHPONDS

**13.** The Tram Terminus until it was extended to Staple Hill in 1905. This view of the busy centre of Fishponds. The Full Moon Hotel can be seen between the two trams. Card posted in Fishponds June 1916.

**14.** Devon Road, now known as North Devon Road. Published by Guillion, a local photographer, and was posted in January 1908. St. Mary's Church Spire just visible.

**15.** New Station Road leading to the Railway and Fishponds Station, with Coronation Avenue, the turning on the left of the picture.

**16.** The beginning of New Station Road, at the junction with Fishponds Road. The card published by Guillion, and written from No. 3 in 1907, shows the tram shelter, with the conductor and driver awaiting passengers.

17. Cheapside, Fishponds. The tram en route to Fishponds and Staple Hill from Zetland Road, via Old Market. The trees behind removed in 1934 for shops and the Post Office to be built, when Beechwood House, home of the Robinson family was demolished. Card posted in May 1923. Published by Garratt.

18. Fishponds Road, a view 10 years earlier looking in the opposite direction to the above picture. An early taxi cab parked on the left, and a delightful group of children standing in the road. Card posted 17th May 1913.

19. Hillfields Park, a council house estate built in the 1920's-early 1930's. Beechen Drive reached at the top of the Causeway.

20. Woodland Way, new council houses on the border of Fishponds and Kingswood, between Thicket Avenue and Soundwell Road.

21. Hillfields Avenue leading to Woodland Way in the late 1920's.

22. Briar Way. Children playing in the road, near the junction of Forest Road.

**23.** Fishpond Park looking along part of Manor Road, with large houses facing the park and St. Mary's Church. Note the early lamp in the middle of the junction, an interesting feature in 1914 when the card was posted. A Garratt card.

**24.** The Park towards Manor Road on the left, with shops in middle distance. Posted locally in 1915 from Maywood Crescent.

**25.** The War Memorial, with wreaths and flowers remembering the dead of the first world war, taken for the Armistace Day of November 11th, in the early 1920's. Card by Garratt. Published in the York Series.

DR. BELL'S SCHOOL, FISHPONDS.

**26.** This view of Dr. Bells School at Fishponds in the 1930's. The Fishponds School was founded in 1850. Andrew Bell (1753-1832) started a new idea in teaching, with older boys teaching the younger boys.

27. Hannah Mores Cottage. Hannah More was born in this cottage on February 2nd 1745. She was famous for her writings and dramatic associations in the theatre. She knew Garrick, and in Bristol in 1799, she married Zachary Macauley. She lived for a time at Barley Wood in Wrington and started a school with her sisters in Park Street, Bristol. She died in 1833, and is buried with her sisters in Wrington Church, Somerset.

28. Elfin Road, situated at the junction with Oldbury Court Road, a road with nearly all its houses having venetian blinds. Card published by Garratt.

# FISHPONDS

Holy Trinity Bazaar Hannah Moore Bristol. 7/4/15

**29.** Hannah More's fame spread far from Fishponds. She founded schools in other districts of Bristol and nearby villages. Although this is not actually a school of her own founding, the Church of England recognised her educational influence sufficiently to apply her name (here mis-spelled Moore) to the school that it built in 1835 opposite the then recently erected Holy Trinity Church in Trinity Road, St. Philips, Bristol.

The school survived until the 1960's when the buildings were demolished to provide part of the site for constructing the new District Police Station.

**30.** Fishponds Rangers Amateur Football Club, taken about 1910. The two small boys look keen supporters.

# FISHPONDS

**31 & 32.** Carnivals were held in Vassel Park Estate, the children performing Morris Dancing. The two postcards form a part of a series which all relate to the Carnival held in the 1920's.

# FISHPONDS

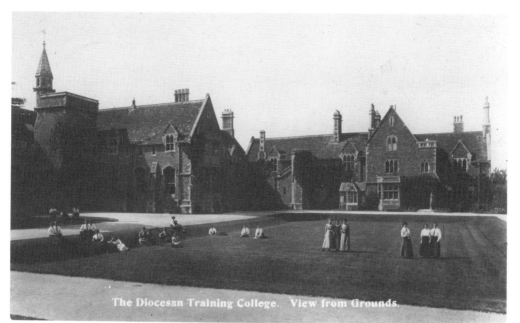

The Diocesan Training College. View from Grounds.

**33.** The Diocesan Training College near Oldbury Court Road, trained women for the teaching profession. The card published by L. Skuse of Fishponds, and written by student Vera to her mother in Oxford in 1916.

**34.** A group of young women students attending the college. Note the mascots in front of the girls.

**35.** Beaufort War Hospital, now Glenside Hospital, during the 1914-18 war. The hospital was used for treating casualties of the war. This postcard shows the fine entrance and clock tower of the main building. A Viner card.

**36.** Beaufort War Hospital. Soldiers along the main drive, some in wheelchairs. Behind several buildings which made up the Beaufort Hospital, and are all part of Glenside Hospital today. A Viner card.

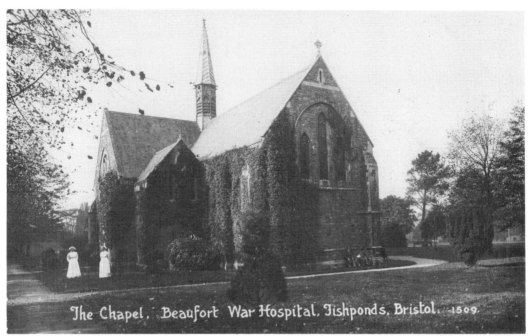

37. The Chapel, Beaufort War Hospital. The ivy clad chapel with trees surround it, a place for quiet moments, with four soldier patients sitting on the wall, and two nurses posing for the photographer. A Viner card.

38. Beaufort War Hospital. M.C. Ward, with most of the soldiers in the picture having had a limb amputated.

39. Beaufort War Hospital. The Laundry. A superb social history picture, with sheets being pressed, with adequate protection for the workers from the machinery. Note the baskets and tiled walls.

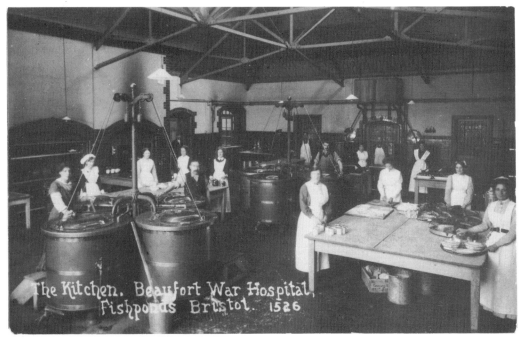

40. Beaufort War Hospital. The Kitchen. Again a superb picture with the many staff busy preparing food, with large boilers for cooking of vegetables. Note the scrubbed table.

# FISHPONDS

41. Looking towards the park from the "Straits", the large bay window houses on the left, one with wooden scaffolding. Card postally used 1916.

42. The opposite direction towards the picture above, with the Unionist Club on the left, the trees of the park beyond, with Manor Road to the left.

**43.** A view of All Saints Church, with iron railings surrounding it. A Garratt card.

**44.** Pountney's Pottery. The potteries adjoining Lodge Causeway, renowned the world over for fine china. Moved to this site from St. Phillips Marsh in 1906, finally closing in early 1970's. Posted in 1912.

45. Vassels Estate of Oldbury Court, the house in the middle distance, a large mansion owned by the Vassel family. The mansion is now demolished, and the estate is a public park. Card postally used 1914.

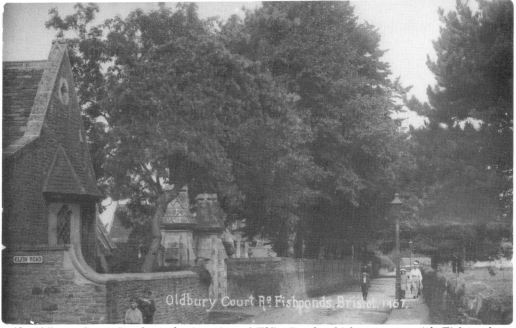

46. Oldbury Court Road, at the junction of Elfin Road, which connects with Fishponds Road. Message of greetings from Cecil and Joyce, posted from Oldbury Court Road in October 1916.

**47.** South Parade also known as the Straits, looking towards the Cross Hands Hotel. Children shading their eyes in the bright sunlight whilst the photographer took the picture.

**48.** Looking in the opposite direction towards the park. Tram lines visible from Staple Hill. Card posted in 1911.

# FISHPONDS

49. Cross Hands Hotel at the junction for Downend and Staple Hill. The Hotel built in 1904. Card posted from Fishponds in 1923.

50. Another view of the Straits, showing a double kerb to the pavement. A summer scene, showing many trees, later removed for road widening and the building of shops.

**51.** The cobbled road, with a tram en route from Staple Hill. The lamp standard in the road marking the junction. Posted in 1908.

**52.** The road to Downend shortly after the junction with the Cross Hands Hotel, note the spelling of Downend on the postcard. Another card published by Milton's Fishponds.

53. Looking towards Fishponds, with tram no. 151 picking up passengers. The Regal Cinema, with its dome adjoining the turning for Pendennis Road.

54. In the opposite direction, the tram line now a single track. The ornate iron porch on the shop, middle right, is still there today.

55. An earlier view looking down the High Street. The card postally used in 1916, shows a varied selection of shops. Note the large gas lamps outside the shops.

56. Tram no. 145 en-route to Staple Hill, just about to leave the double track. Advert can be seen for Pratts Motor Spirit, and Perth Dye Works.

**57.** High Street connecting with Broad Street, with Victoria Street the turning on the left, and Soundwell Road to the right by the Portcullis Hotel.

THE PICTURE HOUSE, STAPLE HILL.     *Proprietor* Herbert F. Wren.    Xmas, 1927.

**58.** The Picture House in 1927 when showing silent films, seen in this view with the dome removed, the proprietor Herbert F. Wren. Later converted to talking films. Building used today for Bingo.

High St. Staple Hill.

Hamilton, Photo. Staple Hill.

**59.** Another early view looking towards Fishponds on the corner of Victoria Street, the Fir Tree Off License on the corner with its advert for Georges & Co. Pale Ales and Cold Beers. Card by Hamilton, posted in 1904.

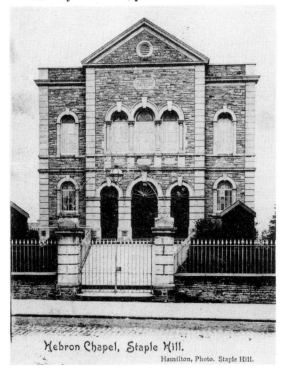

Hebron Chapel, Staple Hill.

Hamilton, Photo. Staple Hill.

**60.** Hebron Chapel situated just beyond the shops on the right of picture no. 59, set back from the main road. Card by Hamilton of Staple Hill. Posted in 1906.

**61.** A late view of the Cross Roads between High Street and Broad Street, posted in 1954. The Fir Tree Off License seen in picture 59 now an Estate Agent, traffic lights now control the junction.

**62.** The first few shops in Broad Street showing the variety of architecture in Staple Hill. Card postally used in 1906.

**63.** Soundwell Road which connects Two Mile Hill Road with High Street. The car no. H.W. 5239 found no trouble in parking. Card postally used 1916.

**64.** South View in the early 1930's leading to Park Road, and the main road at Broad Street.

**65.** Broad Street at the junction with Teewell Hill. A winter scene published by Viners of Bath. The tram on double track approaching the Staple Hill terminus.

**66.** A view further along towards the junction with High Street. A single shop adjoining the cottages on the right, with adverts for Wills Star Cigarettes, and for Blue Bell Tobacco, also Wills Woodbines.

# STAPLE HILL

**67.** The main gates of Page Park named after Alderman Arthur Page who gave the land. Card posted in Fishponds in 1915. Published by Viner of Bath.

**68.** A view inside the park with the large pond, with the pavilion and clock tower in the distance. Posted from Staple Hill in 1914.

*You get the Lake replaced, we will keep it Clean we would require at least 6 inches of water and give model exhibitions from all Type of Radio Control Ships a (Models only)*

# DOWNEND

69. The centre of Downend, showing a row of cottages, with the Scout Memorial in front, erected in memory of the Rev. P.G. Alexander Member of the 1st Downend Scout Troop, unveiled in 1921. Card published by Hepworth. Postally used in 1926.

70. The same view as picture no. 69, but taken in the 1950's with shops, an early zebra crossing and traffic islands.

# DOWNEND

**71.** The cricket field adjoining Christ Church, known as W.G. Grace Memorial, bought by Downend Cricket Club in 1920. The pavilion on the right opened by Mrs. Dunn formerly Grace, in memory of her brother in 1922.

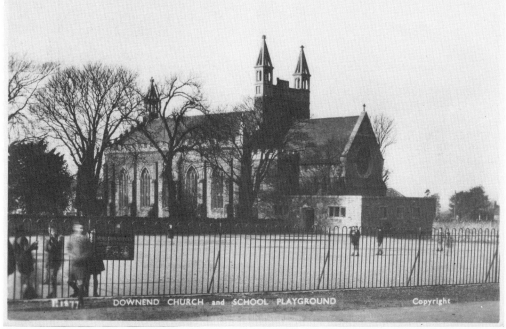

**72.** Christ Church Downend. The children playing in the playground attended Downend National School.

# DOWNEND

**73.** Cleeve Road. A view of the original cottages, published by the Downend Press, and posted in April 1939. This road connects Badminton Road with Westerleigh Road.

**74.** This view looking towards the road connecting Cleeve Hill with Bromley Heath Road. Card posted in 1947. The latter is now a very busy road, with new houses built.

# DOWNEND

75. Downend Road, the main road from Fishponds, taken in the early 1920's. The horse and cart waits outside the Beaufort Hunt Public House, while the owner partakes a tipple perhaps. Card by Hepworth.

76. North Street at the junction with Pleasant Road and Hermitage Road, known in the 1880's as Staple Hill Road. Card in the York Series. Posted in 1920.

**77.** The chalet bungalows of Peach Road were built in the 1920's, known locally as Chilvern Cottages, the road connects with Westerleigh Road.

**78.** Cleeve Lawns off Cleeve Hill Road in the 1950's. Message on the postcard reads "These houses only cost £4,500, you'd like it here."

# DOWNEND

79. The front entrance to Cleeve Hill House, owned by the Cave family from 1859 to the early 1900's. The Cleeve Hill Estate was sold for development in 1920.

80. Cleeve Hill House used as a hospital for soldiers injured during the first world war 1914-1918. Here patients relax in the snow, throwing snowballs!

81. Cleeve Hill Hospital, the patients and nurses in the snow, taken on the same day as picture no. 80, with more snowballs about to be thrown. Both pictures taken by Hamilton of Staple Hill.

82. The cottage homes at Downend were built on land given by Sir Charles Cave in 1901. There were fourteen cottages, giving deprived and orphan children a home like atmosphere. In 1963 they became a girls school, before finally being demolished for housing development in 1985.

# DOWNEND

83. Cleeve Hill Road in the years of early development, showing older houses on left, and newer modern houses of the late 20's early 30's beyond. A few trees remaining from pre-development.

BAUGH FARM, DOWNEND.

84. Baugh Farm, one of the largest farms in the Mangotsfield and Downend area, dating back to the 17th century, when it was farmed by Issac Baugh.

85. Badminton Road, the main road leaving Downend towards Yate and Chipping Sodbury, known as Sodbury Road until the 1880's. The Green Dragon Hotel on the right. Motor bike no. D.W. 601 standing by the verge. Taken in the 1920's.

86. Westerleigh Road leading to the village of that name, just south of Coalpit Heath.

# INDEX

ISBN 0 9514648 1 7